The GROSS AND GOOFY Body

You've Got Nerve!

The Secrets of the Brain and Nerves

By Melissa Stewart

Illustrated by Janet Hamlin

mc Marshall Cavendish Benchmark

New York

THIS BOOK WAS MADE POSSIBLE,
IN PART, BY A GRANT FROM THE
SOCIETY OF CHILDREN'S BOOK WRITERS AND ILLUSTRATORS.

Published by Marshall Cavendish Benchmark
An imprint of Marshall Cavendish Corporation

This publication represents the opinions and views of the author based on Melissa Stewart's personal experience, knowledge, and research. The information in this book serves as a general guide only. The author and publisher have used their best efforts in preparing this book and disclaim liability rising directly and indirectly from the use and application of this book.

Other Marshall Cavendish Offices:
Marshall Cavendish International (Asia) Private Limited, 1 New Industrial Road, Singapore 536196 • Marshall Cavendish International (Thailand) Co Ltd. 253 Asoke, 12th Flr, Sukhumvit 21 Road, Klongtoey Nua, Wattana, Bangkok 10110, Thailand • Marshall Cavendish (Malaysia) Sdn Bhd, Times Subang, Lot 46,
Subang Hi-Tech Industrial Park, Batu Tiga, 40000 Shah Alam, Selangor Darul Ehsan, Malaysia

Marshall Cavendish is a trademark of Times Publishing Limited

All websites were available and accurate when this book was sent to press.

Library of Congress Cataloging-in-Publication Data
Stewart, Melissa.
You've got nerve! : the secrets of the brain and nerves / by Melissa Stewart.
p. cm.—(The gross and goofy body)
Includes index.
Summary: "Provides comprehensive information on the role the brain and
nerves play in the body science of humans and animals"—Provided by publisher.
ISBN 978-0-7614-4157-1
1. Nervous system—Juvenile literature. I. Title.
QP361.5.S74 2010
612.8—dc22
2008033560

Editor: Joy Bean
Publisher: Michelle Bisson
Art Director: Anahid Hamparian
Series Designer: Daniel Roode

Photo research by Tracey Engel
Cover photo: Blend Images/Alamy

The photographs in this book are used by permission and through the courtesy of:
Alamy: Science Photo Library, 18. *Getty Images:* The Image Bank/Pal Hermansen, 5 (bottom); Stone/Wendy Ashton, 7 (top); Taxi/Nick Clements, 8; Dorling Kindersley, 9 (top); Photographer's Choice/Cecile Lavabre, 11; Riser/Jenny Acheson, 12; 3D4Medical.com, 13 (top); National Geographic/George Grall, 13 (bottom); Photographer's Choice/Colin Anderson, 15; Photonica/Allison Michael Orenstein, 16; The Image Bank/Paul Taylor, 19 (top); National Geographic/Brian Skerry, 20; Photographer's Choice/Tom Walker, 21 (left); Iconica/Jamie Grill, 22; Digital Vision/Ken Wramton, 23 (right); Photographer's Choice/Jim Cummins, 30; Dorling Kindersley/Jane Burton, 31 (bottom); National Geographic/Joel Sartore, 35 (bottom); Stone/Everard Williams, 36; Dorling Kindersley/Peter Anderson, 38; The Image Bank/Jeff Rotman, 39 (bottom); Photolibrary/London Scientific Films, 39 (top); Photographer's Choice/Harald Sund, 40. *Photo Researchers, Inc:* Hybrid Medical, 14.

Printed in Malaysia (T)
135642

CONTENTS

FOOD FOR THOUGHT

A grapefruit.

A walnut.

A piece of cauliflower.

A stick of warm butter.

Put them together, and what do you get? Nope, not a tasty after-school snack. You get a clearer picture of your body's control center—your brain.

Your brain is the size of a large grapefruit, and it's shaped sort of like cauliflower. Its surface is wrinkled like a walnut, and it feels soft and squishy, like warm butter.

Your brain is connected to 30,000 miles (50,000 kilometers) of **nerves** that snake through your body like strings of licorice. The nerves carry millions of messages to and from your brain every second—even when you're asleep. Good thing, too. Your life depends on it. You'll be amazed at all the ways a brain and nerves make life better for you—and for other animals, too.

Lift arm

Blink eye

A chemical inside a chipmunk's brain slows its heartbeat and breathing in autumn, when the animal goes into **hibernation**.

A magnetic material inside the brains of sea turtles, birds, and butterflies acts like a compass. It helps the animals stay on course as they **migrate**, or travel long distances.

YOUR BODY'S BOSS

What lets you read, run, and rhyme, as well as count, chew, and climb? What lets you laugh, love, and leap, as well as smell, smile, and sleep? What lets you dream, draw, and drink, as well as taste, talk, and think?

Your brain, of course! From wiggling your toes to scratching your nose, your bossy brain controls just about everything you do.

No computer on Earth is as powerful as your brain. It sends out about 6,000,000,000,000 messages every minute. And it can store up to 1,000,000,000,000,000,–000,000,000 bits of information. Not bad for a wrinkly, 3-pound (1.4-kilogram) lump that's 78 percent water and 10 percent fat!

Breath of Life

Your brain needs a steady supply of oxygen to do its job. That's why breathing is so important.

Go just ten seconds without oxygen, and you'll faint. If you stopped breathing for ten minutes, you'd probably die.

Lost His Mind

The world-famous physicist Albert Einstein died in New Jersey in 1955. A doctor removed his brain so people could study it. But the brain got lost. Someone finally found it in a cooler in Kansas in 1978.

Welcome to Kansas

FRAGILE

BRAIN BOOSTERS

Which uses up more energy—running a race or taking a test? Seem like a no-brainer? Don't answer too fast. Sometimes working your brain takes more fuel than working your body.

Your brain uses up to 25 percent of all the **nutrients** that come from your food. So, if you want to think right, you need to eat right.

To improve your memory, eat egg yolks, liver, milk, and soybeans. Want to think quickly? Try salmon, almonds, and seeds. To stay alert, eat nuts, fish, chicken, beef, eggs, cheese, and yogurt. What's the most important meal of all? Breakfast.

After a night with no food, your brain needs fuel. But don't just eat sugary cereal. Boost your brainpower with whole-grain toast or oatmeal and high-protein foods such as eggs, peanut butter, or yogurt.

Beating the Heat

Feeling groggy? Recharge your brain with a big yawn.

Turning nutrients into energy produces heat. And when your brain warms up, it slows down.

Yawning pulls extra air into your body, and that makes blood flow faster. As the blood travels around your brain, it picks up the extra heat and carries it away.

9

GET THE MESSAGE?

Ever sniff a whiff of your brother's sweaty socks? Ugh! Disgusting!

It's just one of the many things your body's neurons, or nerve cells, sense every day. The stinky stench triggers a warning message that races from one **sensory neuron** to the next at 150 miles per hour (241 kilometers per hour), all the way to your brain.

Each neuron has dozens of branched **dendrites** that receive information from neighboring neurons and carry it to the **cell body**. Then the message enters a long **axon** that passes the information to other neurons.

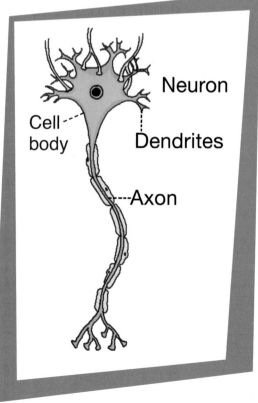

Neuron

Cell body

Dendrites

Axon

As soon as your brain receives and processes the smelly sock alert, it sends out a new message telling your body how to respond. Traveling at more than 200 miles per hour (322 kph), **motor neurons** whisk the information to the muscles in your mouth and fingers.

That's when you yell, "Pee-eeew!" and your fingers squeeze your nostrils shut.

Phew, what a relief!

Brain Pain

Ever sucked down a frozen drink too fast? Ouch! That hurts!

No one knows what causes "brain freeze." But pain sensors in the roof of your mouth may be to blame. Some scientists think they send out messages when they cool too quickly.

PRACTICE MAKES PERFECT

Today, riding your bike is no big deal. But remember the first time you tried?

You had to learn so many things all at once—pedaling, steering with the handlebars, and staying balanced. You had to watch the road, listen for cars, and know how to hit the brakes. It was pretty hard, right?

But as you practiced, riding your bike got easier and easier. Ever wondered why?

It's because the neurons in your brain don't touch one another. There's a gap, or **synapse**, between the axon of one neuron and the dendrite of the next neuron. When a message reaches a

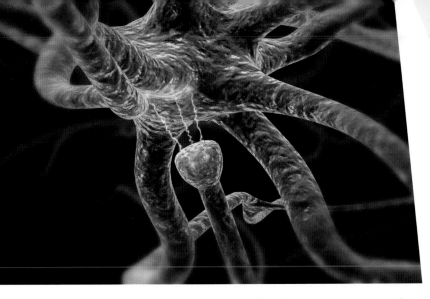

A computer illustration showing a synapse and information being sent across the gap.

synapse, the axon releases a chemical that carries information across the gap.

When you try something new, wide synapses separate the neurons that need to transmit messages to and from the brain. But as you practice, your dendrites grow, and the gaps shrink. Eventually, messages have no trouble moving from neuron to neuron. And as messages whiz back and forth along familiar pathways, riding your bike starts to seem simple.

System Shutdown

How does a Mohave rattlesnake stop **prey** in its tracks? The poison flowing out of its fangs shuts down the chemicals that carry messages across synapses. And if the victim's nerves can't work, neither can anything else.

NOT JUST NEURONS

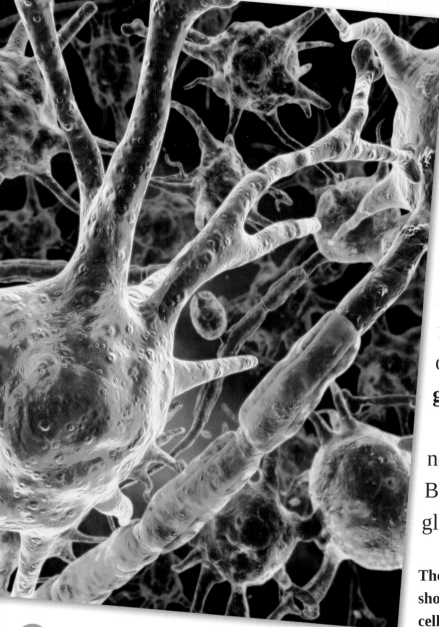

Think about the last time you stubbed your toe. Yow, that hurt!

But pain wasn't the first thing you felt. An instant earlier, you felt a tiny bump.

Why do some nerve messages travel faster than others? Because you've got **glial cells**.

You have 100 billion neurons inside your brain. But there are even more glia—ten times more.

The glial cells in this computer image are shown in all colors of the rainbow. But the glial cells inside your body are pinkish white.

Scientists used to think the tiny cells didn't do much, but now they know better. Glia surround neurons and hold them in place. They remove nutrients and oxygen from your blood vessels and feed nearby neurons. Glia even destroy nasty germs.

Glia also wrap around some axons like blankets. The spaces between these itty-bitty insulators are called **nodes**. As messages move along an axon, they jump from node to node.

Axons coated with glia transmit information hundreds of times faster than bare axons. That's why some kinds of nerve messages reach your toes faster than others.

Going, Going, Gone

Most of your cells live a few hours, days, or weeks. But some brain cells last a lifetime— and that's lucky for you. Once they're gone, you can't replace them.

A microscopic image of brain cells.

YOUR THINKING CAP

Sometimes people say, "Put on your thinking cap." But the truth is, you never take it off.

Even though your brain's uppermost layer—the **cortex**—is as thin as a pancake, it processes most of the information that enters your brain. It does all your thinking and decision making. It sorts through messages from your five senses and tells your muscles how to react. It even understands what other people are saying and plans what you'll say in response.

Wondering how your cortex can do so much? Well, it's not really as small as it seems. If you could flatten out all its crinkly creases, your cortex would cover an area the size of a pillowcase.

What causes all those ridges and grooves? The network of nerves created by your thoughts and memories. And, believe it or not, that network is completely unique.

Nobody else experiences all the things you do. And nobody has exactly the same feelings. So nobody's cortex looks the same as yours.

What's in a Name?

How is your cortex like the bark on a tree? It's rough and bumpy. In fact, *cortex* is the Latin word for "bark."

19

GOT GROOVES?

Humans, chimps, dolphins—they're some of the smartest animals around. But why?

Sure, they have big brains. But whales have even bigger brains, and they aren't nearly as smart. So size isn't everything.

Humans, chimps, and dolphins also have big brains in comparison to their total body size. Scientists have studied brain-to-body ratios in many different creatures, and here's what they've found:

Most **predators** have larger brain-to-body ratios than the animals they eat. That's how they outsmart their prey. Fruit-eating animals have larger brain-to-body ratios than leaf eaters—probably because it takes extra brainpower to tell when fruit is ripe.

But hold on. That's not the whole story. It turns out hummingbirds have a larger brain-to-body ratio than humans. Do you think they're smarter than us? No way! Birds, reptiles, and even some mammals have smooth cerebral cortexes—no ridges and valleys or dark, hidden alleys. That means they have less space for the complex nerve networks that make you so smart.

Walnut-sized brain

Miniminds

Stegosaurs may have been the most brainless animals ever to live. The 2-ton (1,814 kg) dinosaurs were more than 30 feet (10 meters) long, but some scientists think their brain was the size of a walnut.

21

TAKING SIDES

Not everyone in your class learns the same way.

Many kids learn best by reading, listening to the teacher, or taking notes. But some students need to see or experience things for themselves.

Which kind of learner are you? The answer will tell you something about your brain.

Even though no two cortexes look exactly alike, they all have a deep groove running down the middle. It splits the brain into two **hemispheres**.

Your left hemisphere is more logical. It's in charge of reading, writing, math, and language. And it controls the muscles on the right side of your body.

Your right hemisphere is more creative and artistic. You use it to understand shapes and forms. It controls your feelings and

Left side:
Reading
Writing
Math
Language

Right side:
Creative
Artistic

Think It Through

Many artists are left–handed. Can you explain why?

sense of humor. And it sends signals to muscles on the left side of your body.

Everybody uses both sides of their brain. But most people depend on one hemisphere more than the other.

If you learn best by reading, listening, or taking notes, your left hemisphere rules. But if you need to see or experience things to really understand them, your right brain is boss.

LOVE THOSE LOBES

No part of your brain works all on its own, but scientists divide your cortex into four **lobes**. Each area controls a few important functions.

See the words on this page? Thank your occipital lobe. It receives and processes information from your eyes.

Hear a friend calling your name? That's because your temporal lobe is hard at work. It collects and analyzes sound messages and understands words.

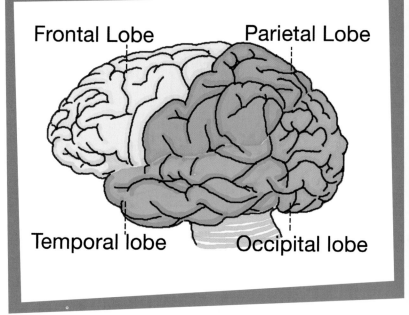

Frontal Lobe

Parietal Lobe

Temporal lobe

Occipital lobe

Did you rat out your brother the last time he told a lie? You did if your frontal lobe told you to. It makes all your decisions and solves problems, too.

Which tastes worst: liver or Brussels sprouts? Your parietal lobe knows. It processes taste messages. It also sorts through touch, pressure, and pain signals flooding in from all over your body.

Cerebral Clues

Today it's easy to see the brain at work. But long ago the only hints came from people with head injuries.

• A soldier shot in the back of the head lost his vision.

• After a man bashed the front of his head during a fight, he didn't know the difference between right and wrong.

• When a woman fell off a horse and hit the side of her head, she couldn't hear.

THAT MAKES SENSE!

Today we know a lot about the brain and how it works. But for thousands of years people all over the world thought the heart—not the brain—was the center of thoughts and feelings.

In the 1660s, when settlers were pouring into what later became America's thirteen colonies, the respected British thinker Henry More said the brain showed "no more capacity for thought than a cake of suet or a bowl of curds."

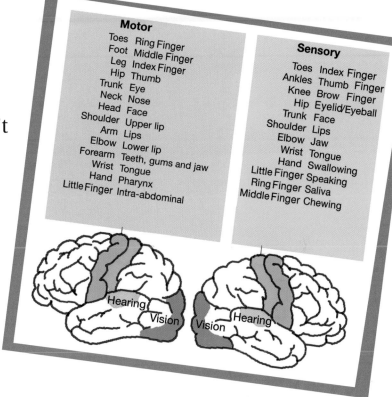

Sounds silly, right? But it wasn't until the 1950s that the American brain surgeon Wilder Penfield discovered which areas of the brain control each part of our bodies.

4000 BCE to 1397 BCE Ancient India
Believed the heart, not the brain, was the center of thinking and **consciousness**.

3100 BCE to 31 BCE Ancient Egypt
Believed the heart, not the brain, was the center of feelings and intelligence.

1100 BCE to 146 BCE Ancient Greece
Believed the soul was located in the brain.

146 BCE to 476 CE Ancient Rome
Some thinkers suggested that the brain controlled emotion, wisdom, knowledge, sense, justice, reason, understanding, and dreams. Others disagreed.

610 CE to 1400 CE Early Islamic Cultures
Recognized that the brain receives, processes, and reacts to information from the five senses, but thought the heart was the center of thinking and decision making.

Love riddles and brain teasers? So does your brain. What about sudoku puzzles, crossword puzzles, and word finds? All these mental exercises help keep your mind at the top of its game.

But to really whip your body's boss into tip-top shape, try physical exercise, too.

That's right. Whenever you run a race, jump rope, or ride your bike, you're boosting your brainpower. Scientists have discovered that after exercising, your mind is more settled. You

feel better, and you can focus your attention more easily. And that can help you learn. Your body may even release chemicals that can repair damaged neurons.

So, the next time you're having trouble with your homework, take a break for a game of soccer or baseball. Afterward, doing math problems or remembering spelling words might seem a whole lot easier.

Needle-y Nerves

You're wide awake, but your foot sure isn't. It feels numb and lifeless. What's going on?

When nerves get squashed, they can't send messages to your brain. And your foot "falls asleep."

When you stand up, your foot will tingle. It might even burn. But in just a few seconds, everything will be back to normal.

DON'T STRAIN YOUR BRAIN

Why can you drink a glass of water without spilling it? Why can you run without falling down? Why can you catch a baseball?

Because you have a cerebellum. It's just below the hairline on the back of your head.

To see your cerebellum in action, try this:

- Run down a flight of stairs as fast as you can.

- Now go down the stairs again. But this

time, think about every move you make. Watch how your knees bend and your toes flex. Notice where each foot lands.

When you think about your movements, you can't go down the stairs nearly as fast. That's because thinking gets your cerebrum involved.

Most of the time your cerebellum takes charge of familiar movements. Using a steady stream of information from your eyes and ears, it can quickly understand your body's position and actions. Then it sends out messages that coordinate your movements.

Sizable Cerebellums

Why is a bird's cerebellum large compared to the rest of its brain? Because flying takes a lot of balance and coordination.

A cat's cerebellum is big, too. That's why a cat moves so gracefully and always lands on its feet.

What would your brain look like if you were a fish or a frog? Take a look at your thumb.

That's right, your body's boss would consist of a thumb-sized brain stem with three little lobes—a cerebrum, a cerebellum, and a structure to control your eyes.

In fact, it wasn't until mammals appeared, about 200 million years ago, that cerebellums grew larger and cerebrums expanded and developed cortexes.

That means earlier animals didn't do much thinking. They spent their time just trying to survive. Today, your brain stem is still in charge of your body's most basic functions.

As part of your brain stem, your **medulla** controls your heart and other muscles that work automatically. Without a medulla, you couldn't breathe, swallow, or digest food. It also decides when you'll cough, sneeze, hiccup, and yawn.

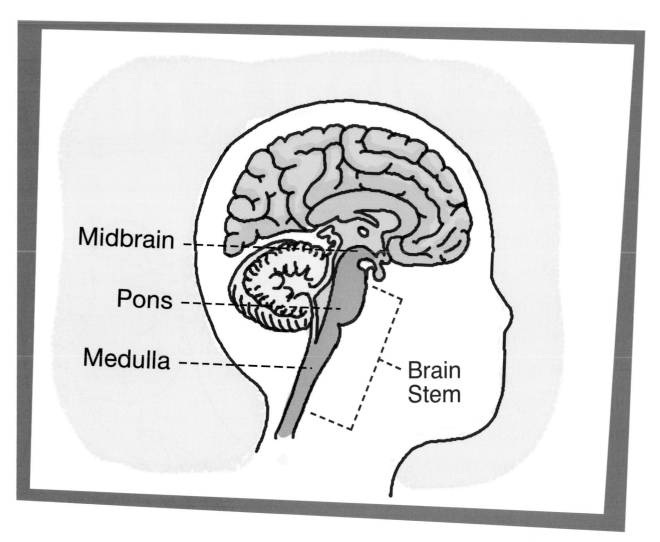

Midbrain

Pons

Medulla

Brain
Stem

Can you feel the socks on your feet? You can now that your cerebrum is thinking about them. But before that, you didn't even notice them. That's because your **pons** was doing its job—sorting through all the messages entering your brain and filtering out the unimportant ones. Your pons also creates dreams and controls some phases of sleep.

Your **midbrain** coordinates head and eye movements and plays a role in hearing.

THE MIDDLE MIND

Smack dab in the center of your head—below your cerebrum, above your brain stem, in front of your cerebellum—there's a cluster of very small structures with very big jobs. Together, they form your brain's limbic system.

The **thalamus** receives incoming sensory information from your ears, eyes, and skin and forwards it to the appropriate area of your cortex.

Your bean-sized **hypothalamus** makes sure that your body always stays the right temperature. It also lets you know when you need food or water or a nice long nap.

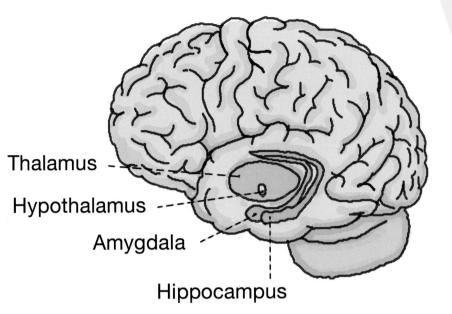

Thalamus

Hypothalamus

Amygdala

Hippocampus

Whether you're feeling sad, scared, or silly, your tiny **amygdala** controls your moods and emotions. It also plays a role in your sense of smell.

Your **hippocampus** receives important information from your cortex and converts it into long-term memories. It also finds places to store memories and helps you retrieve them later.

Un-bee-lievable Brains !

A bee's brain may be small, but it's not so simple. A honeybee's short-term memory lasts as long as a pigeon's and is almost as accurate as a monkey's. That's incredible!

A BUNDLE OF NERVES

Reach around and run your fingertips down your back. Feel that hard, lumpy chain right in the center? It's your **spine**—a series of twenty-six ring-shaped bones.

Your spine surrounds and protects your **spinal cord**—an 11-inch (28-centimeter)-long bundle of nerves that relays messages between your brain and the rest of your body.

All day and all night, sensory messages race up your spinal cord, so your brain understands your surroundings.

At the same time, motor messages zoom down your spinal cord and then branch out along thirty-one pairs of nerves to reach every part of your body. Most of the axons that connect to nearby muscles and organs are just a few inches long, but some stretch more than 3 feet (1 m).

Bypassing the Brain

Your spinal cord is more than just an information highway. It also processes some signals all on its own.

When the wind hurls dirt at you, your spinal cord orders your eyes to snap shut. And if you touch a hot stove, your spinal cord tells your hand to move before the message even reaches your brain. These **reflex** reactions help keep you safe.

SIMPLE MINDS

What do robins and rabbits, lizards and llamas, fish and frogs all have in common? They're vertebrates—just like you.

A vertebrate has a **nervous system** that includes a brain, a spinal cord, and a network of nerves.

But for every vertebrate alive today, there are more than thirty invertebrates burrowing under the ground, whizzing through the air, and swimming in the seas. Most of these spineless creatures have small bodies and simple minds.

- A roundworm's brain has just 300 neurons. A single nerve connects its brain and body.

- A housefly's brain has 300,000 neurons. It also has clumps of nerve tissue that detect and process smells, sounds, temperature, light patterns, pressure, textures, and taste.

- An octopus has a fairly good memory and is capable of learning. Its brain has 300 million neurons and small, lobelike structures.

Brainless Bugs

Without a brain, you'd die in just a few minutes. But a cockroach can run around for weeks with its head cut off. Here's why:

Its neck would seal off long before it bled to death. Clumps of nerve tissue scattered throughout its body control nearby reflexes and movements.

Insects "breathe" through tiny holes in the sides of their bodies.

A cockroach can survive for weeks without food.

IT TAKES NERVES!

As a herd of zebras grazes lazily on the African savanna, a series of short, sharp barks shatters the silence. It's the alarm cry of the herd's leader. He's spotted a hungry lion. As fear surges through the animals' bodies, their nervous systems send out a slew of signals—and their bodies respond.

Teeth stop chewing, and stomachs stop digesting. Hearts pick up their pace, and lungs pull in more air. Cells crank out extra energy, and the animals flee. The zigzagging mass of black and white stripes confuses the lion. Soon, it gives up and wanders away.

Now a new throng of messages rushes through the zebras' bodies. The animals stop running and settle down. Hearts beat more slowly, and lungs take in less air. Teeth start chewing, and stomachs start digesting. Life is back to normal.

Your body responds like a zebra's when you feel scared or excited. It's just one of the many things your body has in common with other animals on Earth.

From keeping us safe and making us laugh to solving problems and creating great works of art, it's hard to believe all the ways our brains and nerves help us every day. And we aren't alone. Many other animals depend on theirs, too.

GLOSSARY

amygdala—The part of the brain's limbic system that controls mood and emotions. It also plays a role in sense of smell.

axon—The part of a neuron that transmits messages to other neurons.

brain stem—The part of the brain that controls your body's most basic functions.

cell body—The central part of a neuron.

cerebellum—The part of the brain that controls balance, coordination, and posture.

cerebrum—The largest part of the brain. It controls thinking, learning, decision making, and more.

consciousness—Awareness of being alive and understanding the world through the five senses.

cortex—The surface of the cerebrum.

dendrite—The part of a neuron that receives messages from other neurons.

glial cell—A tiny cell in the nervous system that supports neurons in a variety of ways.

hemisphere—One of the two halves of the cerebrum.

hibernation—The resting state in which some animals spend the winter.

hippocampus—The part of the brain's limbic system that creates, stores, and retrieves memories.

hypothalamus—The part of the brain's limbic system that regulates body temperature, thirst, hunger, and sleep.

limbic system—A group of small structures in the middle of the brain, below the cerebrum and above the brain stem.

lobe—In the brain, one of four large sections of the cerebrum that is largely responsible for a particular body function.

medulla—The part of the brain stem that coordinates head and eye movements. It also plays a role in hearing.

midbrain—The part of the brain stem that controls your heart and other muscles that work automatically.

migrate—To travel to another place in search of food and more favorable living conditions.

motor neuron—A neuron that carries messages from the brain to muscles and organs.

nerve—A bundle of axons that carries messages to and from the brain.

nervous system—The system that controls and coordinates an animal's body.

node—The part of a nerve that is not surrounded by glia. It is a landing spot for nerve messages.

pons—The part of the brain stem that filters incoming sensory messages so that only essential information is relayed to the cerebrum. It also creates dreams and controls some phases of sleep.

predator—An animal that hunts and kills other animals for food.

prey—An animal that is hunted by a predator.

reflex—A nervous system response controlled by your spinal cord.

sensory neuron—A neuron that carries messages from the sense organs to the brain.

spinal cord—A bundle of nerves protected by the spine. It relays messages between your brain and nerves all over your body.

spine—Backbone; the twenty-six bones that run down the middle of your back.

synapse—The gap between two adjacent neurons.

thalamus—The part of the brain's limbic system that receives incoming sensory information from your ears, eyes, and skin and forwards it to the appropriate area of your cortex.

A NOTE ON SOURCES

Dear Readers,

I probably spent more time researching this book than any other title in this series. The brain is a complicated organ, and scientists are learning new things about it every day. Some of the recent findings include the amazing capacity of a honeybee's memory, and the link between physical exercise and our ability to learn.

Most of the basic information about the parts of the brain and how they work comes from medical or biology textbooks. I also relied on articles in medical journals and popular magazines.

If you use the Internet carefully, it can be a great resource. That's where I discovered how the Mohave rattlesnake kills its prey and tracked down the brain-to-body ratios of many different animals.

Of course, one of the best sources of all is real scientists. I also spoke to several scientists while researching this book. They helped me spot material that was out-of-date and also clarified information about invertebrate nervous systems. I couldn't have written *You've Got Nerve!* without their help.

—Melissa Stewart

BOOKS

Moscovich, Ivan, and Ian Stewart. *The Big Book of Brain Games: 1,000 PlayThinks of Art, Mathematics & Science.* New York: Workman, 2006.

Newquist, H. P. *The Great Brain Book: An Inside Look at the Inside of Your Head.* New York, Scholastic, 2005.

Simon, Seymour. *The Brain: Our Nervous System.* New York: HarperCollins, 2006.

WEBSITES

Get Body Smart: Nervous System

Text and diagrams give a complete overview of our brain, and nervous system.

www.getbodysmart.com/ap/nervoussystem/menu/menu.html

Neuroscience for Kids

This site has simple, clear descriptions and explanations of the brain and nervous system's parts and how they work.

http://faculty.washington.edu/chudler/introb.html

INDEX

Page numbers in **bold** are illustrations.

ABOUT THE AUTHOR

Melissa Stewart has written everything from board books for preschoolers to magazine articles for adults. She is the award-winning author of more than one hundred books for young readers. She serves on the board of advisors of the Society of Children's Book Writers and Illustrators and is a judge for the American Institute of Physics Children's Science Writing Award. Stewart earned a B.S. in biology from Union College and an M.A. in science journalism from New York University. She lives in Acton, Massachusetts, with her husband, Gerard. To learn more about Stewart, please visit her website: www.melissa-stewart.com.

ABOUT THE ILLUSTRATOR

Janet Hamlin has illustrated many children's books, games, newspapers, and even Harry Potter stuff. She is also a court artist. The Gross and Goofy Body is one of her all-time favorite series, and she now considers herself the factoid queen of bodily functions. She lives and draws in New York and loves it.